# More OUTRAGEOUS Crossword Puzzles and Word Games for Kids

**Helene Hovanec**

**Introduction by Will Shortz**

ST. MARTIN'S GRIFFIN
NEW YORK

www.stmartins.com

ISBN 0–312–30062-X

First Edition: August 2002

10 9 8 7 6 5 4 3 2 1

# Introduction

One of my earliest puzzle-related memories as a child is of arranging letters like this:

$$A \quad R \quad C \quad F \quad S$$
$$R \quad I \quad O \quad A \quad I \quad A$$
$$T \quad M \quad D \quad B \quad N \quad X \quad W$$

Every combination of three touching letters here, reading from top to bottom, spells a word—starting on the left with ART, ARM, AIM, AID, RIM, RID, ROD, and so on, continuing over to SIN, SIX, SAX, and SAW on the far right.

What would compel me to do this I don't know. But games of this sort have helped foster a lifetime love of words. They build vocabulary, broaden knowledge, and sharpen the brain, besides being fun.

Like me, Helene Hovanec—a lifetime friend and the author of this book—has been a "puzzlehead" since she was a child. Her puzzles twist and sharpen the brain as all good puzzles do. In addition, as you'll see in the following pages, she incorporates riddles and jokes into them as well. So not only do you feel a sense of satisfaction when you complete her puzzles, you may have a smile or laugh, too.

And anything that gives us a sunny smile or laugh I'd call a good thing!

—WILL SHORTZ
Crossword Editor of *The New York Times*

# How to Solve
## by Helene Hovanec

Every puzzle is a little game between you, the solver, and me, the puzzle maker. I've hidden something in each puzzle for you to find. Think of yourself as a detective who is collecting clues, one by one. When you find all of them, you've solved the case! In this book, the solution is often the answer to an outrageous riddle that will make you laugh or groan.

**For crosswords:** Read each clue and, if you know the answer, write the word into the grid either going across or down. If you don't know the answer, just skip that clue and go on to another one. Most people start with 1 Across, but you can start with any clue. There's no right or wrong way to solve a crossword. After you've solved the puzzle, you might have to do something else to find the riddle answer. Sometimes you'll have to read the circled letters from left to right and top to bottom. At other times you'll have to place letters from numbered spaces into the same numbered blanks below the grid. Always be sure to match up the numbers in both places.

**For word finds:** Circle each word very carefully, because the letters that you don't use will be important. You'll have to place those letters into blank spaces to find the answer to the riddle. When you're searching for the unused letters to write into the blanks, go from left to right and top to bottom and be sure not to skip any letters.

**For fill-ins:** Think of this puzzle as a type of jigsaw. Each word in the list fits into just one space in the grid. Always start with a letter that is already written in the grid. Count the number of boxes in the word that contains that letter. For example, it could be a 5-letter word that starts with B. There will be one 5-letter word that starts with B in the list. Write that word into the grid and work from there.

If you're stuck on a puzzle and can't go any further, just stop solving and do something else. Have a snack, watch TV, or play a game. When you return, you'll often find that you can solve the puzzle without any trouble. It's as if your brain just needed a break. It's also okay to look up answers in a dictionary, ask someone for help, or even take a peek (just a quick one) at the answers. Just remember to have fun!

# Junk Food

After you finish the crossword, take the circled letters and put them in the spaces below the grid. Go from left to right and top to bottom to answer this riddle:

## What do whales chew?

## ACROSS

1. A sandwich is made with two pieces of __
4. Tell a fib
6. There's usually a __ of soap in the shower
7. Full of dirt (rhymes with BUDDY)
8. The opposite of sell
9. A dog or cat is a house __
11. A sheriff wears this for identification
13. Put into action (anagram of SUE)
15. Horror movie, "Nightmare on __ Street"
16. Flowers often given for Valentine's Day

## DOWN

1. Nickname for Robert
2. Opposite of late
3. Really stupid
4. Young boy
5. Country whose capital is Cairo
8. Sacred book
9. Many swimmers use __ in their ears to keep out water
10. The back of an area is called the __
12. Not well-lit (rhymes with HIM)
14. The 19th letter of the alphabet

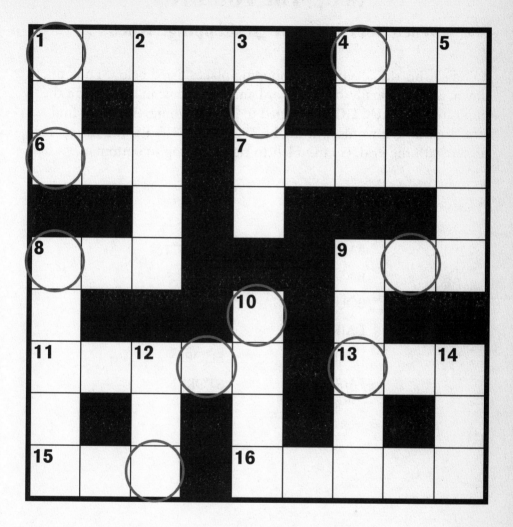

🐝 **Riddle Answer:**

___ ___ ___ ___ ___ ___ ___   ___ ___ ___

# Shop Till You Drop

## When does a battery go shopping? When . . .

To finish this riddle, circle 14 shopping places listed below. Look up,
down, and diagonally, both forward and backward, in the grid on the
opposite page. AUCTION is circled to get you going. After you find
and circle all the words, put the LEFTOVER LETTERS into the spaces
underneath the grid. Go from left to right and top to bottom.

AUCTION            FLORIST

BAKERY             GROCERY

BAZAAR             MALL

BOUTIQUE           MARKET

DAIRY              SALON

DELI               SHOP

FAIR               STORE

```
B A Z A A R I A F
O I U D E R O T S
U F E C T R E U A
T L N S T K O U L
I O L D R I T O O
Q R F A S H O P N
U I M I M J U N I
E S G R O C E R Y
C T E Y R E K A B
```

🐛 **Riddle Answer:**

\_\_ \_ \_\_\_ \_\_\_ \_\_

\_\_ \_\_\_\_

# Missing in Action

Fill in the missing letters in the grid below to make regular words reading across and down. Then move the filled-in letters to the identically numbered spaces below the grid to answer this riddle:

## What did the worm say to the fisherman?

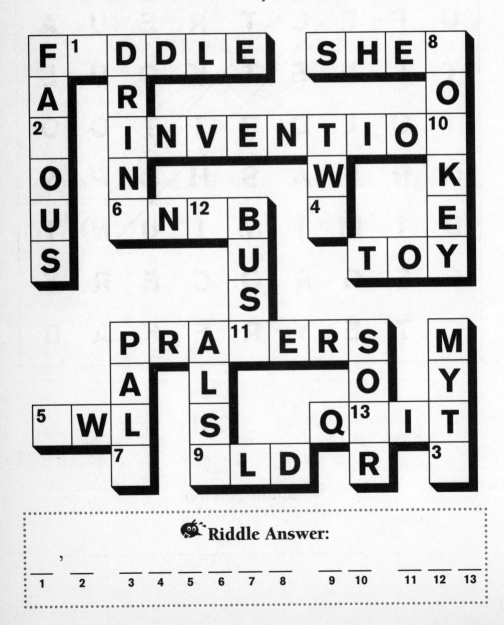

🐛 **Riddle Answer:**

\_\_ , \_\_ \_\_ \_\_ \_\_ \_\_ \_\_ \_\_ \_\_ \_\_ \_\_ \_\_ \_\_
1   2    3  4  5  6  7  8    9  10   11  12  13

# Joking Around #1

Fill in the blanks on each line to spell the name of something associated with math. Then read down the starred column to answer this riddle:

**What practical jokes do math teachers play?**

```
               *
ESTIM _ TING
    FO _ MULA
     D _ GIT
   SUB _ RACTION
  GRAP _
  DECI _ AL
    R _ MAINDER
  MUL _ IPLICATION
    PE _ CENT
   DIV _ SION
  FRA _ TION
   UN _ NOWN NUMBER
 MEA _ UREMENT
```

# Down In The Dumps

### Why is a revolving door so sad? Because everyone. . .

To finish this riddle, put the words on this page into the grid on the opposite page in alphabetical order. Then read DOWN the starred column to find a three-word answer.

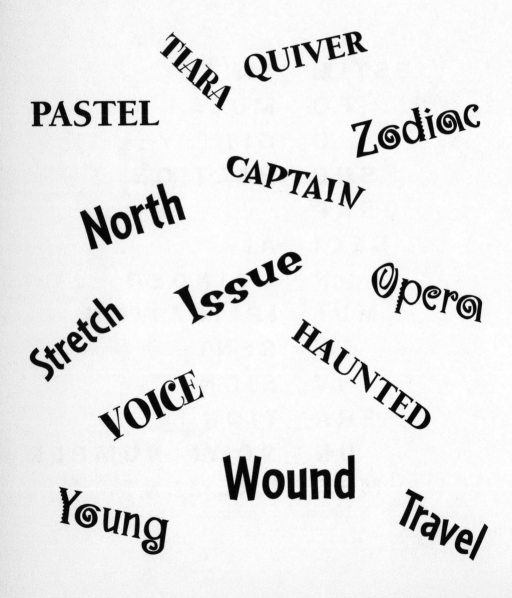

TIARA

QUIVER

PASTEL

Zodiac

CAPTAIN

North

Issue

Opera

Stretch

HAUNTED

VOICE

Wound

Young

Travel

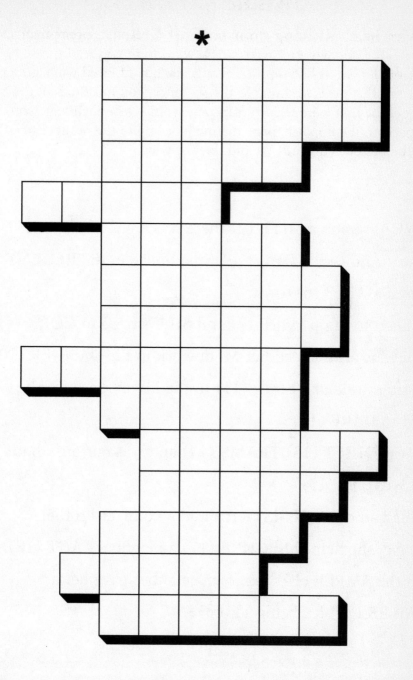

# Annie's Gram

Annie's gram likes to write anagram stories for Annie. Gram changes the letters of one word to make a new word. Can you read the story she wrote for Annie? To do this, change each bold-faced word into a new word that gives meaning to the sentence. You must use all the letters of the first word to form this new word. Write each new word in the space on the opposite page that matches up to the number in ( ) after the bold-faced word. We did one for you.

**CONE** (1) upon a **MITE** (2) there was a girl whose **MEAN** (3) was Annie. She **DEVIL** (4) in a house in the **RECENT** (5) of a **MALLS** (6) town.

She liked to jump **PORE** (7) and **SILENT** (8) to **CORK** (9) music. She also helped her Mom work in the **DANGER** (10). She often walked a **LIME** (11) to the library because she loved to **DARE** (12).

She was **QUIET** (13) **TRAMS** (14) and was curious about new **NIGHTS** (15).

She had an older **RESIST** (16) and a younger brother.

One day she helped **SECURE** (17) a neighbor's **ACT** (18) from the **AMPLE** (19) tree. Her neighbor gave her a **DRAWER** (20) for being so brave.

1. <u>ONCE</u>
2. _____
3. _____
4. _____
5. _____
6. _____
7. _____
8. _____
9. _____
10. _____
11. _____
12. _____
13. _____
14. _____
15. _____
16. _____
17. _____
18. _____
19. _____
20. _____

# Eggs-Citing?

Fill in the grid with words that answer the clues, both Across and Down. Next, fill in the numbered spaces below the grid with the letters that are written in the matching numbered squares. Then, read across to answer this riddle:

## What do you call a funny book about eggs?

## Across

1. In the Middle Ages knights wore metal coverings called __
4. Not me
6. Use this to row your boat
7. Was fond of
8. A carpenter keeps tools in a __
9. Snickers is a popular candy __
11. The funniest person in the circus is usually the __
13. Opposite of tell
15. Very close relative
16. Each and __

## Down

1. It happened a long time __
2. Type of badge for a Boy Scout
3. An actor wants a __ in the movie
4. Talk and talk and talk (also the name of an animal)
5. Not above
8. Hits with the foot, like a soccer ball
9. Step on the __ to stop the car
10. Half of twice
12. Possess
14. A lock opener

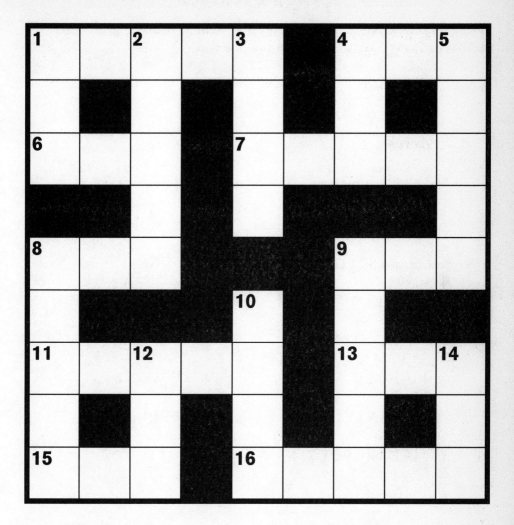

🐝 **Riddle Answer:**

$\overline{\phantom{x}}_{1}$ $\overline{\phantom{x}}_{4}$ $\overline{\phantom{x}}_{6}$ $\overline{\phantom{x}}_{7}$ $\overline{\phantom{x}}_{8}$ $\overline{\phantom{x}}_{9}$ $\overline{\phantom{x}}_{10}$ $\overline{\phantom{x}}_{12}$ $\overline{\phantom{x}}_{14}$

# Sports Scramble

Unscramble the name of each sport and write it into the grid either Across or Down. We did the first one for you.

| Across | Down |
|--------|------|
| 2. CHARYER | 1. BLOATFOL |
| 4. ROCCSE | 3. GOWIRN |
| 6. FASTLOBL | 5. ISKGIN |
| 7. SHAQUS | 7. GWISNIMM |
| 9. NOGIBX | 8. CHOYEK |
| 10. FOLG | 9. LOWGNBI |
| 12. NINEST | 11. SERFBIE |
| 14. LARCSOES | 13. LOPO |

# Extractions

Uh-oh! Someone extracted a three-letter word from each line below and threw it on the opposite page. Your job is to "doctor" the words on this page by replacing those extractions. Take one of the three-letter words and put it in the empty spaces to make a word that fits the definition in the parentheses. Cross off each word as you use it. We did the first one for you.

1. C A N D L E (wax stick with a wick)
2. __ __ __ E S T (wooded area)
3. C O M __ __ __ (war)
4. P A L __ __ __ (king's home)
5. F __ __ __ O R Y (building where goods are manufactured)
6. S W __ __ __ E R (clothing item)
7. S __ __ __ L E T (shade of red)
8. S __ __ __ L Y (not quickly)
9. H O S __ __ __ A L (place for sick people)
10. N E __ __ __ R K (group of TV stations)
11. S T O __ __ __ E (what a closet is used for)
12. T O __ __ __ H E R (not apart)
13. T __ __ __ K L E (shine with quick flashes of light)
14. B R O __ __ __ R (a sibling)
15. S __ __ __ D A L (a disgrace)
16. A R __ __ __ E N T (quarrel)
17. S __ __ __ H E R N (opposite of northern)
18. P E N __ __ __ O N (five-sided figure)
19. P R __ __ __ N T (stop something from happening)
20. S __ __ __ T E R (make popping noises)

| | |
|---|---|
| ACE | GUM |
| ACT | LOW |
| ~~AND~~ | OUT |
| BAT | PIT |
| CAN | PUT |
| CAR | RAG |
| EAT | TAG |
| EVE | THE |
| FOR | TWO |
| GET | WIN |

# Clock Work

After you finish the crossword, take the circled letters and put them in the spaces below the grid. Go from left to right and top to bottom to answer this riddle:

## How do you greet a grandfather clock?

### Across

1. Rubber tubes used for washing cars
4. Part of your mouth
6. Inventor, __ Whitney
7. Holders for fresh flowers
8. The South American country whose capital is Buenos Aires
10. "Where the Sidewalk Ends" is the __ of a book
12. Type of tree
14. A sunbeam
15. Real mean

### Down

1. A tool for weeding
2. Popular item in a playground
3. Eight + nine = __
4. Hollywood is part of __ Angeles
5. Ziti is a form of __
8. Fix clothing (anagram of LATER)
9. Bright thoughts
11. If you don't succeed, __ again
13. The month before June

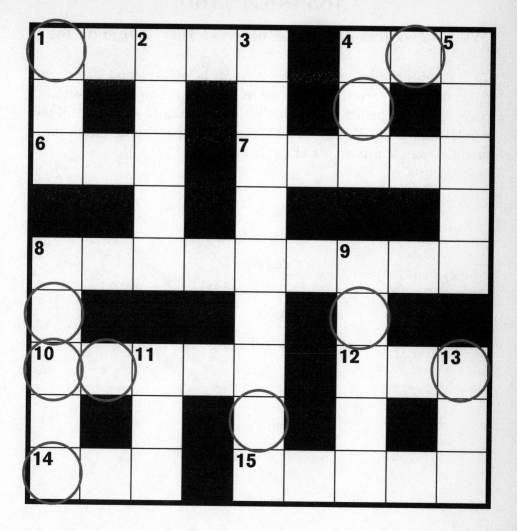

🐝 Riddle Answer:

— — ,  — — — —   — — — — —

# Job Description

## Why are waiters like tennis players? They both have to. . .

To finish this riddle, circle 16 tennis words below. Look up, down, and diagonally, both forward and backward, in the grid on the opposite page. ALLEY is circled to start you off. After you find and circle all the words, put the LEFTOVER LETTERS into the spaces underneath the grid. Go from left to right and top to bottom.

ACE

ADVANTAGE

~~ALLEY~~

BACKHAND

BALL

COURT

DEUCE

FAULT

GRIP

LOB

LOVE

RACKET

SLICE

SMASH

STROKE

VOLLEY

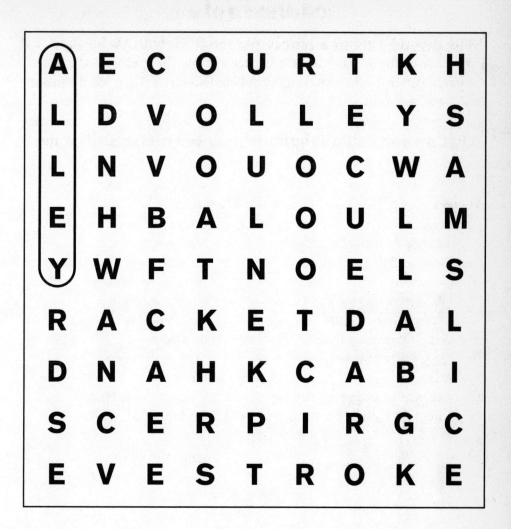

```
A E C O U R T K H
L D V O L L E Y S
L N V O U O C W A
E H B A L O U L M
Y W F T N O E L S
R A C K E T D A L
D N A H K C A B I
S C E R P I R G C
E V E S T R O K E
```

🐛 **Riddle Answer:**

_ _ _ _   _ _ _   _ _

_ _ _ _ _

25

# Stone-Broke

Fill in the grid with words that answer the clues, both Across and Down. Next, fill in the numbered spaces below the grid with the letters that are written in the matching numbered squares. Then, read across to answer this riddle:

## What do you call a Pilgrim who doesn't have any money?

## Across

1. Large animal that lives in the bamboo forests of China
4. Commercials (short form)
6. Uncooked
7. Like someone who's yawning during a long lecture
8. Vehicles used for flying
10. Large body of water, like the Atlantic
12. Two words said at a wedding
14. One of five digits on your foot
15. An occasion

## Down

1. For each (anagram of REP)
2. Not as old
3. Emergency vehicle that takes patients to hospitals
4. What we breathe
5. Coke and Pepsi are soft drinks, or __
8. "They saw a play __ monsters."
9. Opposite of silence
11. December 31 is New Year's __
13. Opposite of in

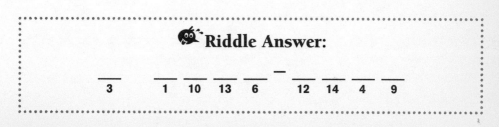

# Fractured English

Put one of the words on this page into one of the blank spaces on the opposite page to make a sentence that makes sense, if you're speaking **fractured English**. Read the sentences aloud for the best groaning effect! Each word will be used once, so you can cross it out when you've placed it in a spot. We did one for you.

ALONE

AUTO

CANOE

CARGO

DEFENSE

DYNAMITE

FORGIVING

HIVE

ICING

~~INTENSE~~

INVEST

LETTUCE

OVERALL

WILLOW

1. The Boy Scouts slept <u>INTENSE</u> at camp.

2. You _____ do your homework before you go out
   to play.

3. _____ come to my house for dinner?

4. _____ in a choir.

5. She _____ lots of money to the store after she
   finishes shopping.

6. How fast does the race _____?

7. Wheeling is a city _____ Virginia.

8. Thank you _____ me a gift.

9. _____ go to the park with us. She'll decide later.

10. The builder put _____ around the pool.

11. They need _____ from the bank.

12. _____ never been on a submarine.

13. Mom will _____ stay up late tonight.

14. The teacher went _____ the tests.

# First/Last

## How does a dog stop a VCR? It presses the. . .

To find the two-word answer that finishes this riddle, do the following:
1. Rearrange the letters of each word on the list to make another **common** word without adding or taking away any letters. Example, POSH can be rearranged to make SHOP.
2. Write the **new** word in the grid on the opposite page. Some words will end at the starred column and others will begin there.
3. Read **down** the starred column.
WARNING: Some words can be rearranged to make two different words. Be sure to choose the correct one.

1. POSH

2. CASE

3. WARD

4. VASE

5. BATS

6. DUES

7. THAW

8. AUNT

9. RIOT

10. STUN

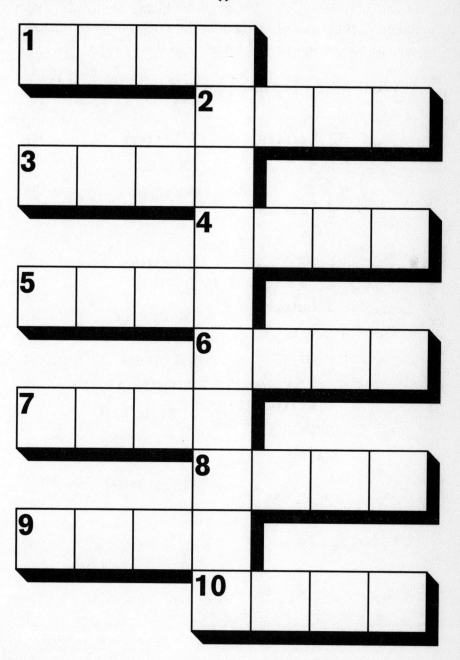

# Dining Out

Put each eating spot into the grid. Use the letters that are already in the grid and work from there. When all the blanks are filled in, take the numbered letters and place them in the same numbered spaces below the grid. Read from 1 to 14 to answer this riddle:

## What kind of eating places do snails avoid?

### 3 Letters
INN

### 4 Letters
CAFE

CLUB

### 5 Letters
DINER

HOTEL

### 6 Letters
BUFFET

EATERY

### 7 Letters
CANTEEN

DRIVE-IN

TEAROOM

### 8 Letters
PIZZERIA

SNACK BAR

### 9 Letters
CAFETERIA

LUNCHROOM

### 10 Letters
RESTAURANT

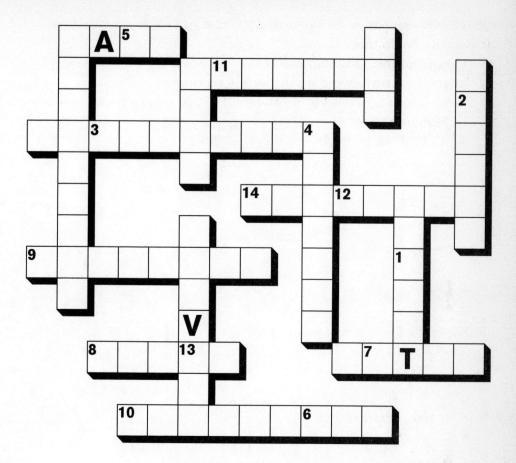

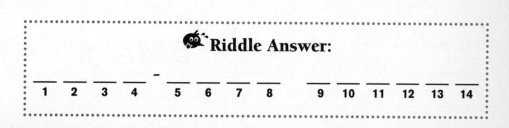

# Do It Yourself

Your do-it-yourself project is to find a riddle and its answer on these two pages. To do this:

    Figure out the answer to each clue

    Write the answer word on the numbered spaces

    Write the same letter on the same numbered space on the
        opposite page

    Work back and forth between both pages

## Clues:

A seven-day period

        27   46   49   13

Cast a ballot on Election Day

        31   51   8   24

Rubber tube for watering grass

        23   44   16   61

Opposite of him

        48   21   50

The "center" of a doughnut

        11   59   52   38

Not happy

        57   30   7

Do this with gum

        36   2   14   19

A person who fibs

        53   12   32   41

Clue (rhymes with mint)

        39   54   60   47

A bird's home

        35   10   25   58

What horses eat

$\overline{\phantom{x}}$ $\overline{\phantom{x}}$ $\overline{\phantom{x}}$
20   28   18

Large sea animal

$\overline{\phantom{x}}$ $\overline{\phantom{x}}$ $\overline{\phantom{x}}$ $\overline{\phantom{x}}$ $\overline{\phantom{x}}$
1   9   17   33   40

A body part with five fingers

$\overline{\phantom{x}}$ $\overline{\phantom{x}}$ $\overline{\phantom{x}}$ $\overline{\phantom{x}}$
37   3   55   5

Shopping wagon

$\overline{\phantom{x}}$ $\overline{\phantom{x}}$ $\overline{\phantom{x}}$ $\overline{\phantom{x}}$
43   34   15   4

What Monopoly and Scrabble are

$\overline{\phantom{x}}$ $\overline{\phantom{x}}$ $\overline{\phantom{x}}$ $\overline{\phantom{x}}$ $\overline{\phantom{x}}$
56   26   45   42   62

A cozy lodge

$\overline{\phantom{x}}$ $\overline{\phantom{x}}$ $\overline{\phantom{x}}$
6   22   29

# Riddle:

___ ___ ___ ___  ___ ___ ___  ___ ___ ___
1   2   3   4    5   6   7    8   9   10

___ ___ ___ ___ ___  ___ ___ ___  ___ ___ ___ ___
11   12   13   14   15    16   17   18    19   20   21   22

___ ___  ___ ___ ___  ___ ___
23   24    25   26   27    28   29

___ ___ ___ ___ ___ ___ ___ ___ ___?
30   31   32   33   34   35   36   37   38

___ ___ ___ ___  ___ ___ ___ ___  ___ ___ ___
39   40   41   42    43   44   45   46    47   48   49

___ ___ ___ ___ ___ ___ ___  ___ ___ ___ ___ ___ ___.
50   51   52   53   54   55   56    57   58   59   60   61   62

# Munchies

Fill in the grid with words that answer the clues, both Across and Down. Next, fill in the numbered spaces below the grid with the letters that are written in the matching numbered squares. Then, read across to answer this riddle:

## What does a small dog eat at the movies?

## Across

1. Jabs with the elbow (rhymes with JOKES)
4. __ Vegas is a city in Nevada
6. "Golly __!" (rhymes with SEE)
7. Opposite of over
8. A holder for peas
9. A slang word for police officer
11. This symbol: ➔
13. The part of your body between the hand and shoulder
15. "This minute! Right __!"
16. Students sit at these in the classroom

## Down

1. A dog with a wrinkled face (rhymes with MUG)
2. Work on dough so it will rise (sounds like NEED)
3. The opposite of sweet
4. A top for a cooking pot
5. Strip of leather attached to a shoulder bag
8. Opposite of fancy
9. Sand creatures that have hard shells (rhymes with GRABS)
10. Had bills to pay
12. Uncooked
14. Title used by some married women (abbreviation)

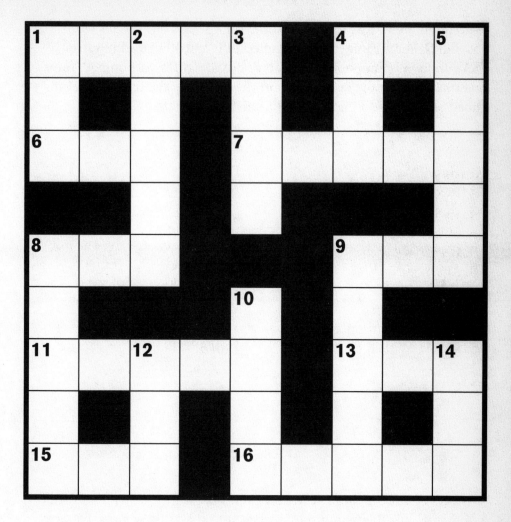

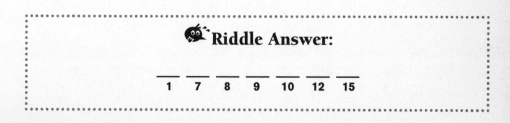

**Riddle Answer:**

___ ___ ___ ___ ___ ___ ___
1   7   8   9   10   12   15

# Making Choices

A homophone is a word that has the same sound as another word, but has a different meaning and is spelled differently. Instead of clues, there are two homophones for each Across and Down number. Your mission is to put the correct one in the grid. Use the letters that are already in the grid PLUS logic* to finish the puzzle

## Across

3. PANE/PAIN
4. HOUR/OUR
8. SELL/CELL
9. IDLE/IDOL
10. AIL/ALE
12. SEEN/SCENE
14. WRAP/RAP
16. STEEL/STEAL
18. RIGHT/WRITE

## Down

1. PEACE/PIECE
2. WHALE/WAIL
5. RAISE/RAYS
6. WEEK/WEAK
7. SALE/SAIL
11. EWE/YOU
12. SIGHS/SIZE
13. KNOWS/NOSE
15. PARE/PAIR
17. AIR/HEIR

*Always count the number of spaces in the grid to see which of the two words fits. Before you put a word into the grid, be sure that any word that crosses with it can also go into the grid.

# Word Mergers

Two related words are merged together on each line. The letters in both words are in their correct order, but they need to be separated. The hint on the left side tells you what to search for. Write the words on the lines. We did the first one for you.

1. RELATIVES

   C O F A T U H S I E R N

   Cousin & Father

2. APPLIANCES

   T O B A S L E N T E R D E R

3. MONTHS

   S E J A P T N E M U A R B E R Y

4. SNACK FOODS

   C P R E H T I Z P E S L S

5. JEWELRY

   B N E C R A C E L E K L A T C E

6. NUMBERS

   N F I N O E T Y R T Y

7. ICE CREAM FLAVORS

   P I V A S N T I L A C H I L A O

8. CIRCUS PERFORMERS

   C A C L O R O W N B A T

9. SANTA'S REINDEER

   C D A O S M H E T E R

10. TIMES OF DAY

    M N I D N I O G H O N T

11. SCHOOL PERIODS

    R L E U C E N S C S H

12. DWARFS

    S B A N S E H F E Z U Y L

# Strike Out #1

Use the grid below and cross out every word that names a vegetable. On most of the lines there will be some extra letters left after you cross out these words. When you're finished, put the LEFTOVER letters in the blanks below the grid. Go from left to right and top to bottom, to answer this joke:

**What do baby sweet potatoes wear when they go to sleep?**

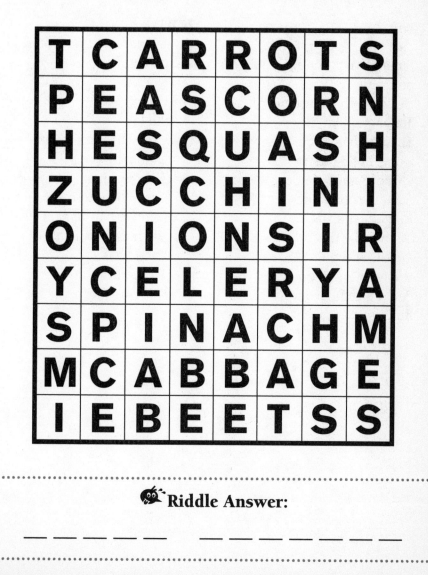

| T | C | A | R | R | O | T | S |
|---|---|---|---|---|---|---|---|
| P | E | A | S | C | O | R | N |
| H | E | S | Q | U | A | S | H |
| Z | U | C | C | H | I | N | I |
| O | N | I | O | N | S | I | R |
| Y | C | E | L | E | R | Y | A |
| S | P | I | N | A | C | H | M |
| M | C | A | B | B | A | G | E |
| I | E | B | E | E | T | S | S |

🐛 **Riddle Answer:**

\_ \_ \_ \_ \_ \_   \_ \_ \_ \_ \_ \_ \_

# Ahoy There!

After you finish the crossword, take the circled letters and put them in the spaces below the grid. Go from left to right and top to bottom to answer this riddle:

## What lives in the water and takes you anywhere you want to go?

### Across

1. "See you __, alligator!"
4. Put a place __ on the table to protect it
6. Dessert with a crust and filling
7. Ten more than fifty
8. The number before two
9. Come in first in a race
11. One of Santa's reindeer whose name is something from outer space
13. We breathe this
15. A male sheep
16. What you might do after you cut yourself (rhymes with SEED)

### Down

1. A baby likes to sit on a parent's __
2. Not those
3. Hurry
4. Stir
5. Use a dressing room to __ __ clothing
8. The grouch on "Sesame Street"
9. Use a loom to make fabric
10. Leftover part of a movie ticket (rhymes with RUB)
12. Dad's wife
14. The color of raspberries

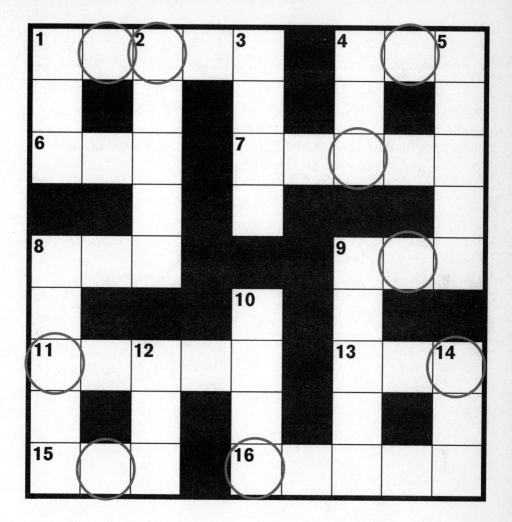

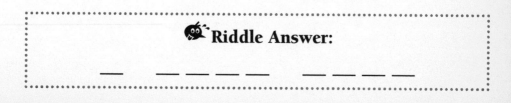

Riddle Answer:

___    ___ ___ ___ ___    ___ ___ ___ ___

# Snowed In

## What snowstorm covered Emerald City?

To find the answer to this riddle, circle the 20 words below that could describe a snowy day. Look up, down, and diagonally, both forward and backward, in the grid on the opposite page. ICY is circled to get you going (and it's crossed off the list). After you find and circle all the words, put the LEFTOVER LETTERS into the spaces underneath the grid. Go from left to right and top to bottom.

| | |
|---|---|
| ARCTIC | FROZEN |
| BITTER | ICELIKE |
| BLEAK | ~~ICY~~ |
| BLUE | NIPPY |
| BRISK | RAW |
| CHILLY | SHARP |
| COLD | SLEETY |
| CRISP | SLUSHY |
| FRIGID | SNAPPY |
| FROSTY | SNOWY |

```
F R I G I D T S H E
R R E T T I B N S B
O A O L I L C O L D
Z W Z S E I Z W E I
E A R A T I C Y E C
N S K C D Y P O T E
I H R S L U S H Y L
P A F Y L L I H C I
P R E U L B R I S K
Y P P A N S C O Z E
```

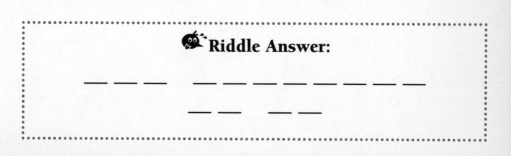

**Riddle Answer:**

\_ \_  \_ \_ \_ \_ \_ \_ \_

\_ \_  \_ \_

# Ugly Parlor

Answer the clues and write the words in the grid going Across or Down. Two clues will form the answer to this riddle:

## What do witches put on their hair?

### Across

1. A baby bear
4. Little Jack Horner said, "What a good boy __ __!"
7. Monkey
8. Frighten (FIRST WORD OF ANSWER)
10. Find on a map (anagram of COT ALE)
12. "__ apple a day keeps the doctor away"
13. Dark shade, __ blue
14. "Hansel __ Gretel"
15. Not you
16. Commercial
17. Frozen water
19. Edges (rhymes with DIMS)
21. "Let's go __ the park"
22. Someone who is well-mannered is __
24. Mist (SECOND WORD OF ANSWER)
26. Not cooked, like salads
27. Use a chair
28. The organ of sight

### Down

1. President Calvin Coolidge's nickname
2. "Once __ a time"
3. Developed into (anagram of MAC BEE)
4. The highest playing card
5. Mommy
6. Middle East country whose capital is Tehran
8. Another name for a pigpen
9. Finish
11. Wide street in a city (abbreviation)
14. Have a high opinion of (anagram of RED AIM)
16. Feel poorly
17. Short form of "it is"
18. Police officers are also known as __
19. __ Rogers was a famous cowboy
20. "Don't leave. __ a little while longer"
22. Nickname for Patrick or Patricia
23. Female lamb
25. Abbreviation for Rhode Island

**Riddle Answer:**

_____ _____

47

# Five 5 X 5's

There are five similar things hidden in each little grid on these two pages. To find them, you'll have to pick one letter from each column, going from left to right. Each letter will be used once, so cross it off after you use it. The category for each grouping is written above the grid. We did the first one for you.

## U.S. Cities

1. **TULSA** _____

2. _____

3. _____

4. _____

5. _____

## Boats & Ships

1. _____

2. _____

3. _____

4. _____

5. _____

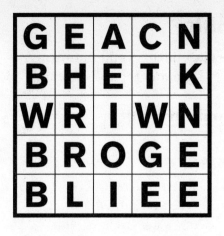

## Colors

1. _____

2. _____

3. _____

4. _____

5. _____

## Fabrics

1. _____

2. _____

3. _____

4. _____

5. _____

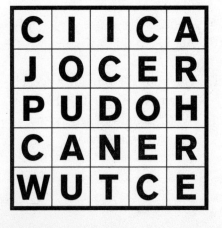

## Drinks

1. _____

2. _____

3. _____

4. _____

5. _____

# Driving Rules

After you finish the crossword, take the circled letters and put them in the spaces below the grid. Go from left to right and top to bottom to answer this riddle:

## What is the speed limit in Egypt?

**Across**

1. Opposite of fast
3. Opposite of beginnings
8. Radical (anagram of REX MEET)
9. Shows that one is sleepy (rhymes with DAWNS)
10. A cook wears this to protect his clothing
11. Opposite of turn off (2 words)
12. Wooden toys used for going down snowy hills
14. Fixes (clothing)
17. Winter is one __ of the year
19. Opposite of always
22. Use a pencil part to rub out a mistake
23. The language spoken in Rome
24. Collections of rainwater
25. Bright colors (rhymes with BEDS)

**Down**

1. Teeter-totters
2. A zoo creature that lives in the water (rhymes with HOTTER)
3. Goes into a voting booth and chooses a candidate
4. The machine that takes the water out of washed clothing
5. An infant who is one day old
6. A cloth that you wrap around your waist (rhymes with HASH)
7. Comic-strip character, __ the Menace
13. A valuable green gem (anagram of MEL DEAR)
14. The day after Sunday
15. Thin cords made of twisted fibers
16. Animals that move very slowly
18. Act like a thief (rhymes with MEAL)
20. Use your __ to make a speech (rhymes with CHOICE)
21. Word called out when you want to be rescued

🐛 **Riddle Answer:**

_ _ _ _ _  _ _ _ _ _

_ _  _ _ _ _

# Lost in Space

Each word on this page has a word that is spelled ALMOST the same on the opposite page. BUT there is one letter that has been lost from the word on the opposite page. The lost letter can be at the beginning, middle, or end of the word and the order of the letters WILL NOT CHANGE. For example, STEED on the opposite page is almost the same as word #1, STEWED, on this page. The letter W has been lost from STEED. Write the lost letter on the blank line next to each word and cross off the word on the opposite page. Then read ONLY the lost letters to find a riddle and its answer.

1.  STEWED    <u>W</u>
2.  CHASES    __
3.  QUAINT    __
4.  BITTER    __

5.  POWDER    __
6.  CHOOSE    __

7.  YEARLY    __
8.  OLIVES    __
9.  PAUPER    __

10. SCARCE    __
11. HURRAY    __
12. BLANKS    __
13. COMPLETE    __

14. WAIST    __
15. DROOPS    __
16. SMELLS    __
17. BEACON    __
18. POINTS    __
19. SNACK    __
20. PLEASE    __

21. WEIGHT    __
22. CHUBBY    __
23. THOROUGH    __

24. GASPED    __
25. JOINTS    __
26. WEAVED    __
27. SHARED    __
28. FLAVOR    __
29. THIRSTY    __

30. DESSERT    __
31. TOASTED    __
32. LAUNCH    __
33. PREACH    __

34. PALACE    __

35. DRAINED    __
36. CLAIMS    __
37. TROPICS    __
38. CHESTS    __
39. FLYING    __

40. SPICES    __
41. LEARN    __
42. LASSOES    __
43. FLAMINGO    __
44. SLICKER    __

| | | |
|---|---|---|
| GAPED | SCARE | QUINT |
| FLING | CHOSE | LIVES |
| FAVOR | WAIT | LUNCH |
| THROUGH | DESERT | CLAMS |
| EIGHT | PINTS | PAPER |
| EARLY | LASSES | CASES |
| DROPS | TOPICS | PLEAS |
| COMPETE | THIRTY | WAVED |
| CHESS | TASTED | SHRED |
| CUBBY | ~~STEED~~ | SELLS |
| BITER | PLACE | SACK |
| BANKS | SPIES | REACH |
| BACON | SLICER | RAINED |
| HURRY | JOINS | POWER |
| FLAMING | LEAN | |

# Travel Problems

Fill in the grid with words that answer the clues, both Across and Down. Next, find the answer words that match the six clue numbers below the grid. Write those words on the blank lines and then read them to answer this riddle:

## What did the hotel manager say to the elephant who couldn't pay her bill?

### Across

1. The comic-strip hero who is also known as Clark Kent
5. Salt __ pepper
8. A paddle for a boat
9. Opposite of in
10. Mistake
11. "Keep __ fingers crossed" (wish for good luck)
12. Opposite of right
13. General Robert E. __ led the Confederate Army during the Civil War
15. Linens that go on a bed
16. Saturn is a __ in the solar system
19. Little "creature" who works with Santa
21. Very eager (anagram of DIVA)
22. You __ your clothes in a suitcase before you go on a trip
25. Large suitcase that's often taken to camp
26. Receive
27. December 24 is Christmas __
28. Small mark (rhymes with JOT)
29. Insects that eat wood (anagram of METER SIT)

### Down

1. A fictional tale
2. Fragrance that has a pleasant smell and is used by women
3. The top of a house
4. A bony growth on a moose's head
5. The month after March
6. Having the least amount of light
7. A city in the state of Washington
14. Sudden onsets of fighting (anagram of TASK CAT)
15. Perspired (anagram of WASTE ED)
17. Opposite of sloppiest
18. Laugh (rhymes with WIGGLE)
20 An apricot is a summer __
23. Leg joints that you bend
24. The part of a plant that holds the flower

## Riddle Answer:

| | | |
|---|---|---|
| 22 Across | 11 Across | 25 Across |
| 5 Across | 26 Across | 9 Across |

# Rink Leader

Fill in the grid with words that answer the clues, both Across and Down. Next, fill in the numbered spaces below the grid with the letters that are written in the matching numbered squares. Then, read across to answer this riddle:

## What do you need to play hockey?

## Across

1. Shines (rhymes with FLOWS)
4. Three is an __ number
6. An adult male
7. A round house found in the Arctic
8. Auto
9. Slippery fish
11. A clan of related people
13. Obtained
15. __ fever is an allergy that causes people to sneeze
16. Not here

## Down

1. Sports section of a school
2. Person who possesses something
3. Type of milk (rhymes with HIM)
4. A night bird that hoots
5. Slobber like a baby (rhymes with COOL)
8. The opposite of throw
9. A bird that is pictured on a quarter
10. A chair or a stool
12. Poison __ could make you break out in a rash
14. What a man might wear around his neck

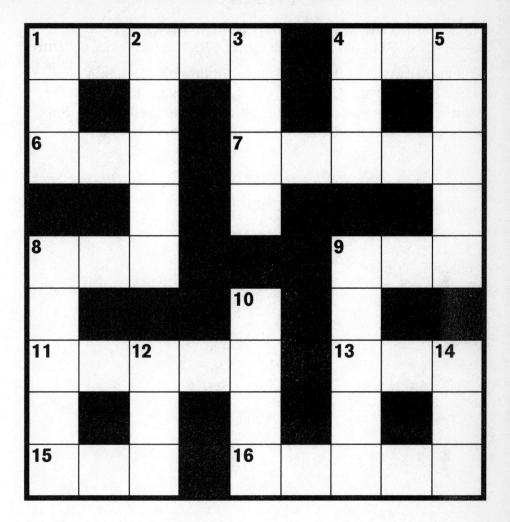

🐛 **Riddle Answer:**

___ ___ ___ ___   ___ ___ ___   ___ ___ ___ ___ ___
 1   2   4   5     7   8   9    10  12  13  15  16

# Yummy!

## What do snowmen eat for breakfast?

To find the answer to this riddle, put each breakfast food into the grid on the opposite page. Use the letters that are already there PLUS the number of letters in each word (or phrase) to guide you. Note: think of the phrases as one word when putting them into the grid.

BREAD

CHEESE

EGGS

ENGLISH MUFFIN

FRENCH TOAST

GRITS

HAM

HOT COCOA

JELLY

OMELET

PANCAKES

WAFFLES

YOGURT

# Riddle of the Middle #1

Write a letter into the middle space on each line to form a common seven-letter word. Then read down the column to answer this riddle:

## Why couldn't Cinderella go snorkeling?

*

```
CRU __ HED
BAT __ TUB
SQU __ EZE

SHA __ LOW
COC __ NUT
MON __ TER
CUS __ ARD

WIT __ OUT
EMP __ ROR
PAT __ IOT

SIN __ LES
BIO __ OGY
GIR __ FFE
COR __ AGE
VER __ ION

MUF __ LER
APP __ AUD
EXH __ BIT
COU __ ONS
SUP __ OSE
JUK __ BOX
HAI __ CUT
```

# Riddle of the Middle #2

Write a letter into the middle space on each line to form a common nine-letter word. Then read down the column to answer this riddle:

## Who does the ocean date?

*

ARCH __ TECT
FROS __ BITE

YOUN __ STER
SEAS __ NING
SEPT __ MBER
INVI __ IBLE

TEMP __ RARY
TURQ __ OISE
GREE __ INGS

FIRE __ ORKS
CONT __ NENT
NIGH __ MARE
GREY __ OUND

QUES __ IONS
PATC __ WORK
PRET __ NDED

HEAR __ ACHE
IMAG __ NARY
WORL __ WIDE
MARV __ LOUS

# Hidden Words

Each sentence has two parts to it: a definition of the answer word and the actual answer word hidden between two or more words. For example: in 1 Across the clue is LOOK and the answer, SEARCH, is hidden between THO<u>SE ARCH</u>ES. After you figure out each word, write it in the grid on the opposite page. Note: the clue and answer can be anywhere in the sentence.

## Across

1. LOOK FOR THOSE ARCHES.
4. MAMA THINKS ARITHMETIC IS FUN.
6. THE HERO ADORES TRAVELING ON THE HIGHWAY.
8. THE KIDS BOUGHT THE BEST OREOS AT THE BAKE SHOP.
9. THE MAN GOT A TROPICAL FRUIT.
10. A SMALL HORSE MIGHT STEP ON YOUR FOOT.

## Down

2. THEY EAT BACON WITH OMELETS AT THEIR HOUSE.
3. A TRIO HAD ICE CREAM WITH REESE'S PIECES BLENDED IN.
5. PARK THE CAB IN A SPOT NEAR THE LOG HOUSE.
7. THEY CAME LATE TO SEE THE DESERT ANIMAL.
8. CLEANING STUFF IS SO APPEALING.

# Detective Work

Fill in the grid with words that answer the clues, both Across and Down. Next, fill in the numbered spaces below the grid with the letters that are written in the matching numbered squares. Then, read across to answer this riddle:

## Who is the most famous dog detective?

### Across

1. Ships that travel underwater (rhymes with RUBS)
3. Bicycle riders wear these to protect their heads
8. More soiled by mud
9. Become ready to be picked, like fruit (anagram of PINER)
10. The meal you usually eat in school
11. Northwestern state whose capital is Salem
12. Clean by scrubbing
14. A brook (rhymes with WEEK)
17. Take a leisurely walk
19. Batman's pal (also the name of a bird)
22. Bookstore Barnes & __ (anagram of B LONE)
23. Chocolate dessert that sounds like a young Girl Scout
24. Short trips to do chores
25. The company that makes the Walkman

### Down

1. Riders sit on these when they go horseback riding
2. Snoopy sometimes pretends that he's the Red __
3. A scary movie is called a __ film
4. Not small
5. Blow up, like a firecracker (anagram of DEEP LOX)
6. What people in choirs do
7. One or the other
13. The tenth month
14. Orange veggie that's often eaten raw
15. The 35th President was John Fitzgerald __
16. Round objects showing models of the earth
18. Huge body of water, like the Pacific
20. A musical instrument similar to a guitar
21. " __ upon a time . . ."

# Frame Up

It's time to relax and solve a "fake" puzzle! It's fake because there are only words on the frame of the grid. Your goal is to fill in the frame with words that match the clues below. Each word shares 1, 2, or 3 letters with the one that comes after it. Start each word in the same space as its clue number. When you get to a corner, follow the direction of the arrow. Since this is meant to be easy, there are more hints for you on the opposite page.

## Clues

1. Sobbed like a baby
2. A magazine worker who fixes articles
3. Flower often found in a corsage
4. Stupid person
5. Not this one, the __ one
6. The main female in an adventure story
7. A bird's home in a tree
8. A baseball pitch that a batter misses
9. This red stuff goes on hamburgers
10. Worried and nervous
11. Breakfast bread
12. Hard metal
13. The little creatures that "work for" Santa
14. A sleeveless garment

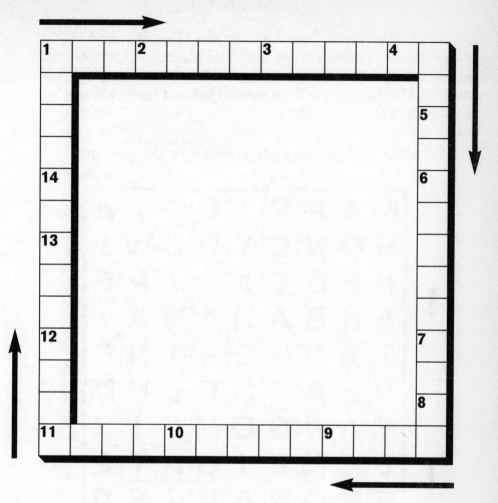

## Hints

1. Rhymes with dried
2. Anagram of RIDE TO
3. Anagram of I CHORD
4. Another word for moron
5. Rhymes with mother
6. Anagram of OH ERNIE
7. Rhymes with best
8. Rhymes with bike
9. You can also put this on French fries
10. Anagram of PEST U
11. Rhymes with coast
12. Rhymes with feel
13. Rhymes with delves
14. Rhymes with rest

# Strike Out #2

Use the grid below and cross out every word that names a fruit. On most of the lines there will be some extra letters left after you cross out these words. When you're finished, put the leftover letters in the blanks below the grid. Go from **right to left** and **bottom to top**, to answer this joke:

**What did the strawberry say to the peanuts?**

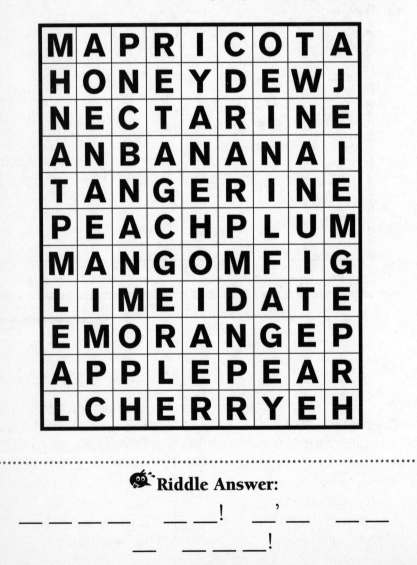

|   |   |   |   |   |   |   |   |
|---|---|---|---|---|---|---|---|
| M | A | P | R | I | C | O | T | A |
| H | O | N | E | Y | D | E | W | J |
| N | E | C | T | A | R | I | N | E |
| A | N | B | A | N | A | N | A | I |
| T | A | N | G | E | R | I | N | E |
| P | E | A | C | H | P | L | U | M |
| M | A | N | G | O | M | F | I | G |
| L | I | M | E | I | D | A | T | E |
| E | M | O | R | A | N | G | E | P |
| A | P | P | L | E | P | E | A | R |
| L | C | H | E | R | R | Y | E | H |

### 🐛 Riddle Answer:

\_\_ \_\_ \_\_ \_\_  \_\_ \_\_!  \_\_'\_\_  \_\_  \_\_ \_\_

\_\_  \_\_ \_\_ \_\_!

# Joking Around #2

Fill in the blanks on each line to spell the name of something that you read. Then read down the starred column to answer this riddle:

## Why do authors work in the basement?

```
          *
      N O _ E
      B R _ C H U R E

      N E _ S P A P E R
    D I A _ Y
    R E C _ P E
    L E T _ E R
      T _ X T B O O K

        _ I O G R A P H Y
    T H _ S A U R U S
    M Y _ T E R Y
      S _ O R Y

      D I _ T I O N A R Y
    P O _ M
    A T _ A S
  N O V E _
    M A G _ Z I N E
    S C _ I P T
    P O _ T C A R D
```

# Ice Is Nice

Ice is such a __ I C E (pleasant) word. And it's found in so many other words. Fill in the blanks on each line with letters to make an "ice" word that fits the definition in the ( ).

1. __ __ __ I C E (something said to someone to tell them what to do)
2. __ __ I C E (the girl who visited Wonderland)
3. __ I C E (cubes used in Monopoly)
4. I C E __ __ __ (refrigerator)
5. I C E __ __ __ __ (country near Greenland)
6. __ __ I C E (fruit drink)
7. __ __ __ __ I C E (honest and fair treatment)
8. __ I C E __ __ __ (a legal document that is needed to drive a car)
9. __ I C E (rodents)
10. __ __ __ I C E (printed message on a bulletin board)
11. __ __ __ I C E (the place where you work)
12. __ __ __ I C E (law-enforcement group)
13. __ __ I C E (what something costs)
14. __ I C E (food often served with beans)
15. __ __ I C E __ (meat-cutting machine)
16. __ __ I C E __ (flavorings used by cooks)
17. __ __ I C E (two times)
18. __ __ __ I C E (Italian city known for its canals)

# Extra! Extra!

The letters in the words in both columns are the same EXCEPT for one extra letter in the column on the left. Write the extra letter on the space in each row. Then read down to answer this riddle.

## What is a crazy young goat called?

DISASTER ___ STRIDES

DIMPLE ___ PILED

PAINTER ___ PARENT

EXPLODE ___ ELOPED

SALUTE ___ TULSA

DENVER ___ NERVE

UMPIRE ___ PRIME

PERSON ___ SNORE

KOSHER ___ HORSE

CERTAIN ___ NECTAR

CRADLE ___ CLEAR

# Tough Situation

After you finish the crossword, take the circled letters and put them in the spaces below the grid. Go from left to right and top to bottom to answer this riddle:

## What should you do if a bull charges you?

### Across

1. Put this on an envelope in the top right corner
4. "How are __ today?"
6. Small rug that's usually at the front door
7. Santa makes these at Christmas (rhymes with FISTS)
8. Glass bottle that holds mayonnaise
9. Narrow bed found in army barracks
11. Animal with antlers (rhymes with GOOSE)
13. The opposite of nothing
15. A bird that gives a hoot
16. Sources of light (rhymes with CAMPS)

### Down

1. The total amount
2. Person who performs in a movie
3. Heap (rhymes with MILE)
4. The opposite of no
5. Queasy, like a stomach
8. Large, like a roll of paper towels (rhymes with GUMBO)
9. Little object on a bracelet
10. Shout
12. Grease
14. Santa Monica is near __ Angeles

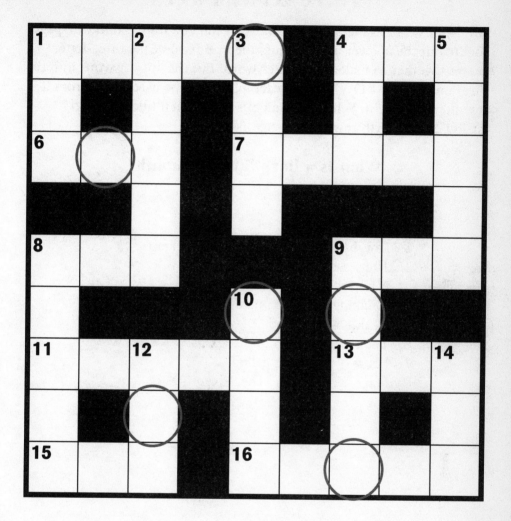

# Three Letter Pieces

All the answers to the clues below are in the box on the opposite page. Figure out the answer to each clue; then put two of the three-letter pieces together to make a six-letter word. Put the answer word into the diagram, writing DOWN. Since each piece will be used once, cross it out after you use it. When all the boxes have been filled in, read ACROSS the fourth row to answer this riddle:

## What is a liar's favorite month?

### Clues

1. Hot drink that adults have at breakfast
2. The season after winter
3. A horse's home
4. A talking bird often named Polly
5. Healthy snack food
6. The country north of the U.S.A.
7. Four __ make one gallon
8. Mark Twain book, "The Adventures of Tom __"

|   | 1 | 2 | 3 | 4 | 5 | 6 | 7 | 8 |
|---|---|---|---|---|---|---|---|---|
|   |   |   |   |   |   |   |   |   |
|   |   |   |   |   |   |   |   |   |
|   |   |   |   |   |   |   |   |   |
| * |   |   |   |   |   |   |   | * |
|   |   |   |   |   |   |   |   |   |
|   |   |   |   |   |   |   |   |   |

| ADA | FEE | ROT | STA |
|-----|-----|-----|-----|
| BLE | ING | RTS | URT |
| CAN | PAR | SAW | YER |
| COF | QUA | SPR | YOG |

# Sky Sores

After you finish the crossword, take the circled letters and put them in the spaces below the grid. Go from left to right and top to bottom to answer this riddle:

## What do you get if you cross a galaxy and a toad?
### Warning: the answer is YUCKY!

## Across

1. Sip a soda with this plastic thing
4. Small bug that sound's like your mom's sister
6. A drink that has its own "bag"
7. Clothing for a girl
8. Put these in your toys to make them work (anagram of TIRE BEAST)
10. Most actors would love to win an Academy __
12. A collie is a long-haired __
14. Have a snack
15. There are 730 days in two __

## Down

1. "Ready, __, go!"
2. __ beef is a popular meat dish at holidays
3. The day after Tuesday
4. President Lincoln's nickname
5. Exams
8. Opposite of cowardly
9. The Asian country whose capital is New Delhi
11. A nickname for Arthur
13. Fuel for a car

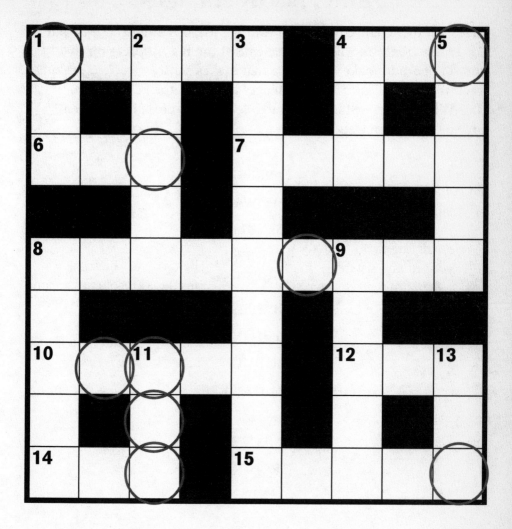

🐛 **Riddle Answer:**

\_\_ \_\_ \_\_ \_\_     \_\_ \_\_ \_\_ \_\_ \_\_

# More Fractured English

Here's another chance for you to ruin the English language! Just put one of the words on this page into one of the blank spaces on the opposite page to make a sentence that makes sense, if you're speaking **fractured English**. Read the sentences aloud for the best groaning effect! Each word will be used once, so you can cross it out when you've placed it in a spot.

ARREST

AVOWAL

BROKER

CANNIBAL

COOKIES

DISTRESS

FELON

HERMIT

LEFTOVER

MAIZE

MISTER

STRETCHER

TOUPEE

WATER

1. The teacher left early. You just _____.

2. The kid _____ the steps and hurt his arm.

3. Dad told us to take _____ before dinner.

4. They _____ an hour ago for the movie.

5. The _____ making a special meal.

6. _____ the fifth month.

7. The catcher put _____ in the locker room.

8. _____ run faster than other animals?

9. She will wear _____ to the party.

10. _____ you doing tonight?

11. He wanted _____ his bill immediately.

12. The runner should _____ legs before the race.

13. On "Wheel of Fortune" a contestant can buy _____.

14. She cried when she _____ favorite doll.

# Musical Comedy

## Why was the turkey asked to join the band?
## Because he. . .

To finish this riddle, circle 19 musical instruments listed below. Look up, down, and diagonally, both forward and backward, in the grid on the opposite page. BANJO is circled to start you off. Cross off each word after you find it. When you have circled all the words, put the LEFTOVER LETTERS into the spaces underneath the grid. Go from left to right and top to bottom.

BANJO

CLARINET

FIFE

GONG

HARP

HORN

KAZOO

LUTE

MANDOLIN

OBOE

ORGAN

PIANO

PICCOLO

PIPE

TROMBONE

TRUMPET

TUBA

VIOLIN

ZITHER

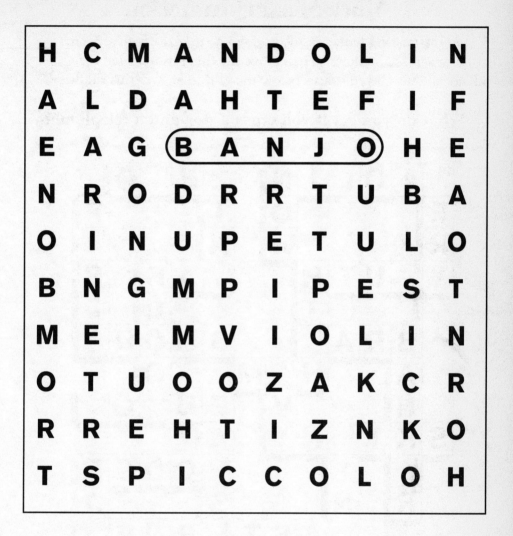

```
H C M A N D O L I N
A L D A H T E F I F
E A G (B A N J O) H E
N R O D R R T U B A
O I N U P E T U L O
B N G M P I P E S T
M E I M V I O L I N
O T U O O Z A K C R
R R E H T I Z N K O
T S P I C C O L O H
```

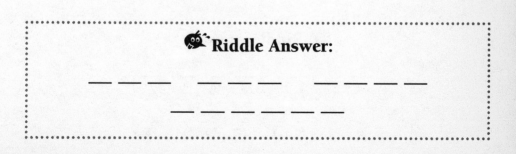

🐝 **Riddle Answer:**

\_ \_ \_   \_ \_ \_   \_ \_ \_ \_

\_ \_ \_ \_ \_ \_

# More Missing In Action

Fill in the missing letters in the grid below to make regular words reading across and down. Then move the filled-in letters to the identically numbered spaces below the grid to answer this riddle:

## What do you get if you cross a dog and a telephone?

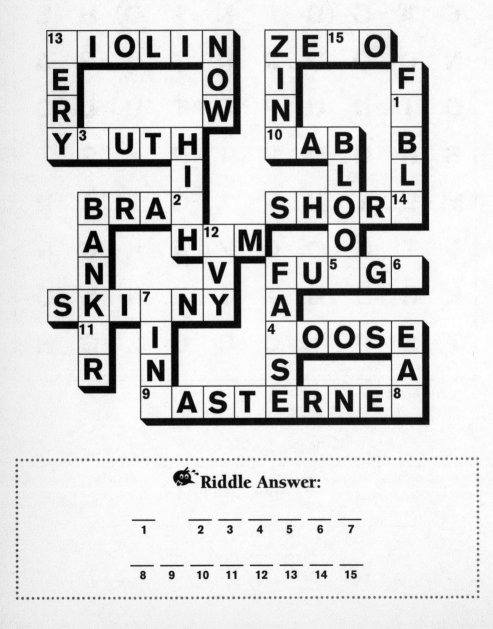

🐛 **Riddle Answer:**

$$\overline{\phantom{x}}_{1} \quad \overline{\phantom{x}}_{2} \; \overline{\phantom{x}}_{3} \; \overline{\phantom{x}}_{4} \; \overline{\phantom{x}}_{5} \; \overline{\phantom{x}}_{6} \; \overline{\phantom{x}}_{7}$$

$$\overline{\phantom{x}}_{8} \; \overline{\phantom{x}}_{9} \; \overline{\phantom{x}}_{10} \; \overline{\phantom{x}}_{11} \; \overline{\phantom{x}}_{12} \; \overline{\phantom{x}}_{13} \; \overline{\phantom{x}}_{14} \; \overline{\phantom{x}}_{15}$$

# Seasonal Fun

Fill in the blank space on each line to name something associated with Christmas. Then read down the column to answer this riddle:

## What should you give an octopus for Christmas?

```
          __ I R E P L A C E
    S T __ C K I N G S
        R __ D O L P H
    C A __ D S

          __ A R T Y
        S __ N T A
        M __ S T L E T O E
        W __ E A T H
          __ L E I G H

        T __ Y S
      G I __ T S

      A N __ E L
      H O __ L Y
    C A R __ L S
      E L __ E S
      T R __ E
          __ T A R
```

# Fashion Plate

Fill in the grid with words that answer the clues, both Across and Down. Next, fill in the numbered spaces below the grid with the letters that are written in the matching numbered squares. Then, read across to answer this riddle:

## What does the 20th letter of the alphabet wear?

**Across**

1. Top floor in a house
4. White powder left in a fireplace (anagram of HAS)
6. A nurse has a first-aid __ in the office
7. Party game, " __ Says"
8. Small musical instrument (anagram of I AM ANCHOR)
10. Samuel __ invented a code
12. Put this small mark over an i
14. Cry
15. The European country whose capital is Madrid

**Down**

1. Noah put pairs of animals on an __
2. Someone who teaches just one person at a time
3. People who buy things in stores
4. Goal
5. A foreign car (rhymes with FONDA)
8. Rounded parts on camels' backs
9. The country next to Nepal
11. Take someone's money illegally
13. A __ is equal to 2,000 pounds

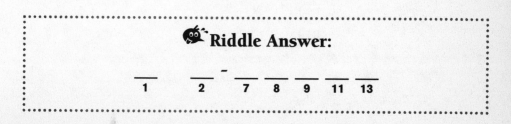

🐝 **Riddle Answer:**

___ ___ - ___ ___ ___ ___ ___
 1      2      7    8    9   11   13

# Just Beastly

Each "beast" will fit into one spot in the grid on the opposite page. Start with the letters that are already in the grid and work from there. When all the words are in the grid, take the circled letters and write them in the blanks below the grid. Go from LEFT to RIGHT and TOP to BOTTOM and you'll answer this riddle:

## Why did the mother skunk take her child to the doctor?
### Warning: This is really a beastly puzzle. It's hard!

## 3 Letters

DOG

ELK

EWE

FOX

GNU

RAT

## 4 Letters

BEAR

LAMB

LYNX

MINK

## 5 Letters

BISON

BURRO

CAMEL

HIPPO

HORSE

HYENA

KOALA

LLAMA

OTTER

SABLE

SHEEP

STOAT

TIGER

## 6 Letters

BADGER

FERRET

RABBIT

## 7 Letters

HAMSTER

## 8 Letters

ELEPHANT

REINDEER

🐛 **Riddle Answer:**

_ _   _ _ _   _ _ _   _ _

_ _ _ _

# Answers

## Junk Food

*Answer:* Blubber gum

## Shop Till You Drop

*Answer:* . . .it runs out of juice

## Missing In Action

*Answer:* I'm hooked on you

## Joking Around #1

ESTIMATING
FORMULA
DIGIT
SUBTRACTION
GRAPH
DECIMAL
REMAINDER
MULTIPLICATION
PERCENT
DIVISION
FRACTION
UNKNOWN NUMBER
MEASUREMENT

*Answer:* Arithmetricks

## Down In The Dumps

*Answer:* . . .pushes it around

## Annie's Gram

1. Once
2. Time
3. Name
4. Lived
5. Center
6. Small
7. Rope
8. Listen
9. Rock
10. Garden
11. Mile
12. Read
13. Quite
14. Smart
15. Things
16. Sister
17. Rescue
18. Cat
19. Maple
20. Reward

## Eggs-citing?

*Answer:* A yolk book

## Clock Work

*Answer:* Hi, old timer

## Sports Scramble

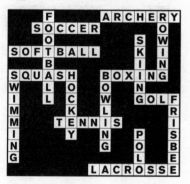

## Job Description

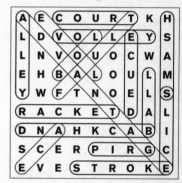

*Answer:* . . .know how to serve

## Extractions

1. Candle
2. Forest
3. Combat
4. Palace
5. Factory
6. Sweater
7. Scarlet
8. Slowly
9. Hospital
10. Network
11. Storage
12. Together
13. Twinkle
14. Brother
15. Scandal
16. Argument
17. Southern
18. Pentagon
19. Prevent
20. Sputter

## Stone-Broke

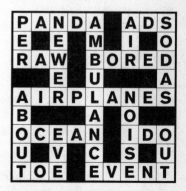

*Answer:* A poor-itan

## Fractured English

| | |
|---|---|
| 1. Intense | 8. Forgiving |
| 2. Auto | 9. Dynamite |
| 3. Canoe | 10. Defense |
| 4. Icing | 11. Alone |
| 5. Willow | 12. Hive |
| 6. Cargo | 13. Lettuce |
| 7. Invest | 14. Overall |

## First/Last

*Answer:* . . .paws button

## Dining Out

*Answer:* Fast-food places

## Do It Yourself

*Clue Answers:*

| | | | |
|---|---|---|---|
| Week | Hole | Hint | Hand |
| Vote | Sad | Nest | Cart |
| Hose | Chew | Hay | Games |
| Her | Liar | Whale | Inn |

*Riddle answer:* What did the hiker
say when he saw an avalanche?
Here come The Rolling Stones.

## Munchies

*Answer:* Pupcorn

## Making Choices

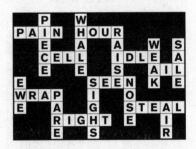

## Word Mergers

1. Cousin & Father
2. Toaster & Blender
3. September & January
4. Chips & Pretzels
5. Bracelet & Necklace
6. Ninety & Forty
7. Pistachio & Vanilla
8. Clown & Acrobat
9. Comet & Dasher
10. Midnight & Noon
11. Recess & Lunch
12. Sneezy & Bashful

## Strike Out #1

*The following vegetables are crossed out (in order):*

Carrots
Peas
Corn
Squash
Zucchini
Onions
Celery
Spinach
Cabbage
Beets

*Answer:* Their yammies.

## Ahoy There!

*Answer:* A taxi crab

## Snowed In

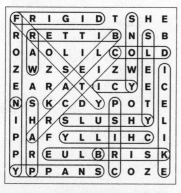

*Answer:* The Blizzard of Oz

## Ugly Parlor

*Answer:* Scare spray

## Five 5x5's

**U.S. Cities**
1. Tulsa
2. Akron
3. Butte
4. Omaha
5. Salem

**Boats & Ships**
1. Canoe
2. Barge
3. Yacht
4. Kayak
5. Ferry

**Colors**
1. Green
2. Brown
3. White
4. Black
5. Beige

**Fabrics**
1. Satin
2. Linen
3. Rayon
4. Denim
5. Suede

**Drinks**
1. Cider
2. Juice
3. Punch
4. Cocoa
5. Water

## Driving Rules

*Answer:* Sixty Niles an hour

## Lost in Space

| | | |
|---|---|---|
| 1. | STEWED | STEED | W |
| 2. | CHASES | CASES | H |
| 3. | QUAINT | QUINT | A |
| 4. | BITTER | BITER | T |
| 5. | POWDER | POWER | D |
| 6. | CHOOSE | CHOSE | O |
| 7. | YEARLY | EARLY | Y |
| 8. | OLIVES | LIVES | O |
| 9. | PAUPER | PAPER | U |
| 10. | SCARCE | SCARE | C |
| 11. | HURRAY | HURRY | A |
| 12. | BLANKS | BANKS | L |
| 13. | COMPLETE | COMPETE | L |
| 14. | WAIST | WAIT | S |
| 15. | DROOPS | DROPS | O |
| 16. | SMELLS | SELLS | M |
| 17. | BEACON | BACON | E |
| 18. | POINTS | PINTS | O |
| 19. | SNACK | SACK | N |
| 20. | PLEASE | PLEAS | E |
| 21. | WEIGHT | EIGHT | W |
| 22. | CHUBBY | CUBBY | H |
| 23. | THOROUGH | THROUGH | O |
| 24. | GASPED | GAPED | S |
| 25. | JOINTS | JOINS | T |
| 26. | WEAVED | WAVED | E |
| 27. | SHARED | SHRED | A |
| 28. | FLAVOR | FAVOR | L |
| 29. | THIRSTY | THIRTY | S |
| 30. | DESSERT | DESERT | S |
| 31. | TOASTED | TASTED | O |
| 32. | LAUNCH | LUNCH | A |
| 33. | PREACH | REACH | P |
| 34. | PALACE | PLACE | A |
| 35. | DRAINED | RAINED | D |
| 36. | CLAIMS | CLAMS | I |
| 37. | TROPICS | TOPICS | R |
| 38. | CHESTS | CHESS | T |
| 39. | FLYING | FLING | Y |
| 40. | SPICES | SPIES | C |
| 41. | LEARN | LEAN | R |
| 42. | LASSOES | LASSES | O |
| 43. | FLAMINGO | FLAMING | O |
| 44. | SLICKER | SLICER | K |

*Answer:* What do you call someone who steals soap? A dirty crook.

## Travel Problems

*Answer:* Pack your trunk and get out!

## Rink Leader

*Answer:* Good ice sight

## Yummy!

*Answer:* Frosted Flakes

# Riddle of the Middle #1

CRUSHED
BATHTUB
SQUEEZE

SHALLOW
COCONUT
MONSTER
CUSTARD

WITHOUT
EMPEROR
PATRIOT

SINGLES
BIOLOGY
GIRAFFE
CORSAGE
VERSION

MUFFLER
APPLAUD
EXHIBIT
COUPONS
SUPPOSE
JUKEBOX
HAIRCUT

*Answer:* She lost her glass flipper

# Riddle of the Middle #2

ARCHITECT
FROSTBITE

YOUNGSTER
SEASONING
SEPTEMBER
INVISIBLE

TEMPORARY
TURQUOISE
GREETINGS

FIREWORKS
CONTINENT
NIGHTMARE
GREYHOUND

QUESTIONS
PATCHWORK
PRETENDED

HEARTACHE
IMAGINARY
WORLDWIDE
MARVELOUS

*Answer:* It goes out with the tide

# Hidden Words

**Across**
1. LOOK FOR THO<u>SE ARCH</u>ES.
4. <u>MA</u>MA <u>TH</u>INKS ARITHMETIC IS FUN
6. THE HE<u>RO AD</u>ORES TRAVELING
   ON THE HIGHWAY.
8. THE KIDS BOUGHT THE BE<u>ST ORE</u>OS
   AT THE BAKE SHOP.
9. THE <u>MAN GO</u>T A TROPICAL FRUIT
10. A SMALL HORSE MIGHT
    STEP <u>ON Y</u>OUR FOOT.

**Down**
2. THEY EAT BACON WIT<u>H OMELE</u>TS
   AT THEIR HOUSE.
3. A TRIO HAD ICECREAM
   WI<u>TH REE</u>SE'S PIECES BLENDED IN.
5. PARK THE <u>CAB IN</u> A SPOT NEAR
   THE LOG HOUSE.
7. THEY <u>CAME L</u>ATE TO SEE THE
   DESERT ANIMAL.
8. CLEANING STUFF IS <u>SO AP</u>PEALING

# Detective Work

*Answer:* Sherlock Bones

# Framed-Up

| C | R | I | E | D | I | T | O | R | C | H | I | D |
|---|---|---|---|---|---|---|---|---|---|---|---|---|
| T |   |   |   |   |   |   |   |   |   |   |   | I |
| S |   |   |   |   |   |   |   |   |   |   |   | O |
| E |   |   |   |   |   |   |   |   |   |   |   | T |
| V |   |   |   |   |   |   |   |   |   |   |   | H |
| L |   |   |   |   |   |   |   |   |   |   |   | E |
| E |   |   |   |   |   |   |   |   |   |   |   | R |
| E |   |   |   |   |   |   |   |   |   |   |   | O |
| T |   |   |   |   |   |   |   |   |   |   |   | I |
| S |   |   |   |   |   |   |   |   |   |   |   | N |
| A |   |   |   |   |   |   |   |   |   |   |   | E |
| O |   |   |   |   |   |   |   |   |   |   |   | S |
| T | E | S | P | U | H | C | T | E | K | I | R | T |

# Strike Out #2

*The following fruits are crossed out (in order):*

Apricot
Honeydew
Nectarine
Banana
Tangerine
Peach
Plum
Mango
Fig
Lime
Date
Orange
Apple
Pear
Cherry

*Answer:* Help me! I'm in a jam!

# Joking Around #2

*
NO<u>T</u>E
BR<u>O</u>CHURE

NE<u>W</u>SPAPER
DAI<u>R</u>Y
REC<u>I</u>PE
LET<u>T</u>ER
T<u>E</u>XTBOOK

<u>B</u>IOGRAPHY
TH<u>E</u>SAURUS
MY<u>S</u>TERY
S<u>T</u>ORY

DI<u>C</u>TIONARY
PO<u>E</u>M
AT<u>L</u>AS
NOVE<u>L</u>
MAG<u>A</u>ZINE
SC<u>R</u>IPT
PO<u>S</u>TCARD

*Answer:* To write best cellars

# Ice Is Nice

| 1. Advice | 10. Notice |
|---|---|
| 2. Alice | 11. Office |
| 3. Dice | 12. Police |
| 4. Icebox | 13. Price |
| 5. Iceland | 14. Rice |
| 6. Juice | 15. Slicer |
| 7. Justice | 16. Spices |
| 8. License | 17. Twice |
| 9. Mice | 18. Venice |

# Extra! Extra!

| DISASTER | A | STRIDES |
|---|---|---|
| DIMPLE | M | PILED |
| PAINTER | I | PARENT |
| EXPLODE | X | ELOPED |
| SALUTE | E | TULSA |
| DENVER | D | NERVE |
| UMPIRE | U | PRIME |
| PERSON | P | SNORE |
| KOSHER | K | HORSE |
| CERTAIN | I | NECTAR |
| CRADLE | D | CLEAR |

*Answer:* A mixed-up kid

## Tough Situation

*Answer:* Pay him

## Three-Letter Pieces

Answers:
1. Coffee    5. Yogurt
2. Spring    6. Canada
3. Stable    7. Quarts
4. Parrot    8. Sawyer

*Riddle answer:* Fibruary

## Sky Sores

*Answer:* Star Warts

## More Fractured English

1. Mister        8. Cannibal
2. Felon         9. Distress
3. Arrest       10. Water
4. Leftover     11. Toupee
5. Cookies      12. Stretcher
6. Maize        13. Avowal
7. Hermit       14. Broker

## Musical Comedy

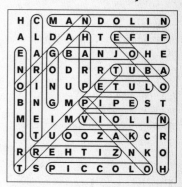

*Answer:* . . . had the drum sticks

## More Missing In Action

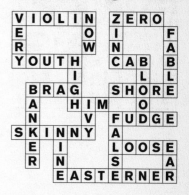

*Answer:* A golden receiver

95

## Seasonal Fun

FIREPLACE
STOCKINGS
RUDOLPH
CARDS

PARTY
SANTA
MISTLETOE
WREATH
SLEIGH

TOYS
GIFTS

ANGEL
HOLLY
CAROLS
ELVES
TREE
STAR

*Answer:* Four pairs of gloves

## Just Beastly

*Answer:* It was out of odor.

## Fashion Plate

*Answer:* A T-shirt